AR 600—43: Conscientious Objection

United States Department of the Army

Army Regulation 600–43

Personnel–General

Conscientious Objection

Headquarters
Department of the Army
Washington, DC
21 August 2006

UNCLASSIFIED

SUMMARY of CHANGE

AR 600-43
Conscientious Objection

This administrative revision, dated 21 August 2006--

o Identifies DODD 1300.6 as the source of implementation (summary statement).

o Updates references (throughout).

o Corrects administrative errors (throughout).

This revision--

o This change establishes uniform standards for processing conscientious
   objector applications during mobilization

o This is a transitional reprint of this publication which places it in the new
   UPDATE format. Any previously published permanent numbered changes have been
   incorporated into the text.

Headquarters
Department of the Army
Washington, DC
21 August 2006

*Army Regulation 600–43

Effective 21 September 2006

Personnel–General

Conscientious Objection

By Order of the Secretary of the Army:

PETER J. SCHOOMAKER
General, United States Army
Chief of Staff

Official:

JOYCE E. MORROW
Administrative Assistant to the
Secretary of the Army

History. This publication is an administrative revision. The portions affected by this administrative revision are listed in the summary of change.

Summary. This regulation establishes uniform standards for processing conscientious objector applications during mobilization. It implements conscientious objectors policy found in DODD 1300.6.

Applicability. This regulation applies to the Active Army, the Army National Guard/Army National Guard of the United States, and the U.S. Army Reserve unless otherwise stated.

Proponent and exception authority. The proponent of this regulation is the Deputy Chief of Staff, G–1. The proponent has the authority to approve exceptions or waivers to this regulation that are consistent with controlling law and regulations. The proponent may delegate this approval authority, in writing, to a division chief within the proponent agency or its direct reporting unit or field operating agency, in the grade of colonel or the civilian equivalent. Activities may request a waiver to this regulation by providing justification that includes a full analysis of the expected benefits and must include formal review by the activity's senior legal officer. All waiver requests will be endorsed by the commander or senior leader of the requesting activity and forwarded through their higher headquarters to the policy proponent. Refer to AR 25–30 for specific guidance.

Army management control process. This regulation contains management control provisions and identifies key management controls that must be evaluated.

Supplementation. Supplementation of this regulation and establishment of command and local forms are prohibited without prior approval from the Deputy Chief of Staff, G–1 (DAPE–ZA), Washington, DC 20310–0300.

Suggested improvements. Users are invited to send comments and suggested improvements on DA Form 2028 (Recommended Changes to Publications and Blank Forms) directly to HQDA, Deputy Chief of Staff, G–1 (DAPE–HRI), Washington, DC 20310–0300.

Distribution. This publication is available in electronic media only and is intended for command levels A, B, C, D, and E for the Active Army, Army National Guard/Army National Guard of the United States, and the U.S. Army Reserve.

Contents (Listed by paragraph and page number)

Chapter 1
General, *page 1*
Purpose • 1–1, *page 1*
References • 1–2, *page 1*
Explanation of abbreviations and terms • 1–3, *page 1*
Responsibilities • 1–4, *page 1*
Policy • 1–5, *page 1*
Noncombatant 1–A–0 inductees or enlistees • 1–6, *page 2*

Chapter 2
Applying for Conscientious Objector Status, *page 2*
Application • 2–1, *page 2*
Advising applicants • 2–2, *page 3*

*This regulation supersedes AR 600–43, 15 May 1998.

UNCLASSIFIED

Contents—Continued

Interviewing applicants • 2–3, *page 10*
Investigating applicants' claim • 2–4, *page 11*
Conducting investigations • 2–5, *page 11*
Review of cases • 2–6, *page 13*
Voluntary withdrawal of application • 2–7, *page 13*
Decision authority • 2–8, *page 14*
Second and later applications • 2–9, *page 14*
Use, assignment, and training • 2–10, *page 15*
Guidelines for processing conscientious objector cases • 2–11, *page 15*

Chapter 3
Disposition of Personnel, *page 16*

Action after approval • 3–1, *page 16*
Discharge of personnel having less than 180 days service • 3–2, *page 16*
Removal of identification as 1–A–0 conscientious objector • 3–3, *page 16*
Separation certificates • 3–4, *page 17*
Expenses • 3–5, *page 17*

Appendixes

A. References, *page 18*

B. Personal Information that Must be Included in Application, *page 19*

C. Suggested Checklist for Processing Conscientious Objector Applications, *page 20*

D. Informal Guide for the Investigating Officer, *page 22*

Figure List

Figure 2–1: Statement of Understanding, Noncombatant Status, *page 4*
Figure 2–2: Statement of Understanding, Privacy Act, *page 5*
Figure 2–3: Statement of Understanding, 38 USC 3103, *page 6*
Figure 2–4: Statement, Waiver of Hearing, *page 7*
Figure 2–5: Statement of Understanding, Hearing on Application, *page 8*
Figure 2–6: Statement, Rebuttal Rights, *page 9*
Figure 2–7: Statement, Waiver of Application, *page 10*

Glossary

Chapter 1
General

1–1. Purpose
This regulation sets forth policy, criteria, responsibilities, and procedures to classify and dispose of military personnel who claim conscientious objection to participation in war in any form or to the bearing of arms.

1–2. References
Required and related publications and prescribed and referenced forms are listed in appendix A.

1–3. Explanation of abbreviations and terms
Abbreviations and special terms used in this regulation are explained in the glossary.

1–4. Responsibilities
a. Deputy Chief of Staff, G–1 (DCS, G–1). The DCS, G–1will—

(1) Develop policies and criteria to classify and dispose of military personnel who claim conscientious objection to participation in war in any form or the bearing of arms.

(2) Establish the Department of the Army Conscientious Objector Review Board (DACORB), which will make final disposition on all cases requesting discharge (1–0) and those requesting noncombatant status (1–A–0) that are not approved by the commands outlined in paragraph 2–8.

b. Commanding General, U.S. Army Human Resources Command (CG, USA HRC) and Commander, U.S. Army Enlisted Records and Evaluation Center (Commander, USAEREC). The CG, USA HRC and the Commander, USAREC will ensure proper disposition of all documents pertaining to the conscientious objector status application in the person's official military personnel file (OMPF) in accordance with AR 600–8–104.

c. Command Staff Judge Advocate (SJA). The Command SJA will—

(1) Thoroughly review the applicant's entire case for sufficiency in law and fact.

(2) Ensure the person's rights have been protected.

(3) Recommend disposition of the case.

1–5. Policy
a. Personnel who qualify as conscientious objectors under this regulation will be classified as such, consistent with the effectiveness and efficiency of the Army. However, requests by personnel for qualification as a conscientious objector after entering military service will not be favorably considered when these requests are—

(1) Based on a claim of conscientious objection that existed and satisfied the requirements for classification as a conscientious objector according to section 6(j) of the Military Selective Service Act, as amended (50 USC, App 456(j)), and other provisions of law when such a claim was not presented before dispatch of the notice of induction, enlistment, or appointment. Claims based on conscientious objection growing out of experiences before entering military service, however, which did not become fixed until after the person's entry into the service, will be considered.

(2) Based solely on conscientious objection claimed and denied on their merits by the Selective Service System before induction when application under this regulation is based on substantially the same grounds, or supported by substantially the same evidence, as the request that was denied under the Selective Service System. Refusal to reopen a person's classification, under the Selective Service System, after his or her entry into service does not have any significance on the merits of a registrant's claim. If views are expressed under the Selective Service System concerning the merits of the claim of a registrant whose beliefs have crystallized after dispatch of his or her induction notice, in connection with a refusal to reopen his or her classification, such expressions must be given no consideration.

(3) Based solely upon policy, pragmatism, or expediency. Applicants who are otherwise eligible for conscientious objector status may not be denied that status simply because of their views on the nation's domestic or foreign policies.

(4) Based on objection to a certain war.

(5) Based upon insincerity.

(a) The most important consideration is not whether applicants are sincere in wanting to be designated as a conscientious objector, but whether their asserted convictions are sincerely held. Sincerity is determined by an impartial evaluation of each person's thinking and living in totality, past and present. The conduct of persons, in particular their outward manifestation of the beliefs asserted, will be carefully examined and given substantial weight in evaluating their application.

(b) Relevant factors that should be considered in determining a person's claim of conscientious objection include training in the home and church; general demeanor and pattern of conduct; participation in religious activities; whether ethical or moral convictions were gained through training, study, contemplation, or other activity comparable in rigor and dedication to the processes by which traditional religious convictions are formulated; credibility of persons supporting the claim.

(c) Applicants may have sought release from the Army through several means simultaneously, or in rapid succession

(medical or hardship discharge, and so forth). They may have some major commitments during the time their beliefs were developing that are inconsistent with their claim. They may have applied for conscientious objector status shortly after becoming aware of the prospect of undesirable or hazardous duty or having been rejected for a special program. The timing of their application alone, however, is never enough to furnish a basis in fact to support a disapproval. These examples serve merely as indicators that further inquiry as to the person's sincerity is warranted. Recommendations for disapproval should be supported by additional evidence beyond these indicators.

b. Care must be exercised not to deny the existence of beliefs simply because those beliefs are incompatible with one's own. Church membership or adherence to certain theological tenets are not required to warrant separation or assignment to noncombatant training and service. Mere affiliation with a church or other group that advocates conscientious objection as a tenet of its creed does not necessarily determine a person's position or belief. Conversely, affiliation with a church group that does not teach conscientious objection does not necessarily rule out adherence to conscientious objection beliefs. Applicants may be or may have been a member of a church, religious organization, or religious sect; and the claim of conscientious objection may be related to such membership. If so, inquiry may be made as to their membership, the teaching of their church, religious organization or sect, as well as their religious activity. However, the fact that these persons may disagree with, or not subscribe to, some of the tenets of their church does not necessarily discredit their claim. The personal convictions of each person will dominate so long as they derive from the person's moral, ethical, or religious beliefs. The task is to decide whether the beliefs professed are sincerely held and whether they govern the claimant's actions in word and deed.

c. The burden of establishing a claim of conscientious objection as grounds for separation or assignment to noncombatant training and service is on the applicant. To this end, applicants must establish, by clear and convincing evidence, that the nature or basis of the claim comes within the definition of criteria prescribed in this regulation for conscientious objection and that their beliefs are sincere. Applicants have the burden of determining and setting forth the exact nature of the request; that is, whether they request separation based on conscientious objection (1–0) or reassignment to noncombatant training and service based on conscientious objection (1–A–0).

d. An applicant claiming (1–0) status will not be granted (1–A–0) status as a compromise. Similarly, discharge will not be recommended for those who apply for classification as a noncombatant.

e. This regulation will not be used to effect the administrative separation of persons who do not qualify as conscientious objectors. Nor will it be used instead of administrative separation procedures such as those provided for unsatisfactory performance, substandard performance of duty, or misconduct, or as otherwise set forth in other Army regulations (AR 600–8–24 or AR 635–200). Under no circumstances will administrative separation of these persons be effected according to this regulation.

f. This regulation does not prevent the administrative elimination, according to law and Army regulations, of any person whose performance of duty after reclassification as a (1–A–0) conscientious objector is substandard or who exhibits another basis for elimination.

1–6. Noncombatant 1–A–0 inductees or enlistees

Persons who were classified (1–A–0) by Selective Service before induction and whose DD Form 47 (Record of Induction) indicates that they are conscientious objectors or who enlisted as (1–A–0) noncombatants for the medical career management field will, upon completion of processing at the U.S. Army Military Entrance Processing Command (MEPCOM), be reassigned to a U.S. Army training center for modified basic training (MBT). These persons must sign and date a counseling statement as set forth in figure 2–1, which will be placed in the person's Military Personnel Records Jacket, (MPRJ, U.S. Army). Upon completion of reception station processing, these persons will be assigned to a basic training company for MBT, which excludes training in the study, use, or handling of arms or weapons as stated in paragraph 2–10*a.* Upon successful completion of MBT, a (1–A–0) classified person will be reassigned to training in the medical career management field. The reporting date to the new unit of assignment will be determined and entered in assignment orders as prescribed in AR 600–8–105. Such persons will not be allowed to avoid the important or hazardous duties that are part of the responsibility of all members of the medical organization. A person who does not meet the requirements for this training, who fails to complete the prescribed course of instruction, or who otherwise cannot be assigned to this duty, will be assigned to other noncombatant duties.

Chapter 2
Applying for Conscientious Objector Status

2–1. Application

a. Military personnel who seek either discharge or assignment to noncombatant duties because of conscientious objection will submit an application on DA Form 4187 (Personnel Action) to their immediate commanding officer. Personnel will indicate whether they are seeking discharge or assignment to noncombatant duties. Applications must also include all of the personal information required by appendix B, and any other information personnel desire to submit. Completion of the foregoing constitutes a formal application. Personnel will date and sign the DA Form 4187 and each enclosure. Nonunit members (Individual Ready Reserve and Standby Reserve) will submit their applications to the oversea area commander or Commander, U.S. Army Human Resources Command–St. Louis (USAHRC–St. Louis), 1 Reserve Way, St. Louis, MO 63132–5200, as appropriate. Applications from recruits will not be submitted to or accepted by MEPCOM or reception stations. For this regulation, the basic training company is considered to be the first duty station for a recruit applying under this regulation.

b. Under normal circumstances, applications from active duty personnel in Active Army units will be processed and forwarded to HQDA within 90 days from the date submitted. Extraordinary circumstances (but *not* routine field exercises) may lengthen this period. If processing time of an application exceeds 90 days, the general court–martial convening authority (GCMCA) will state the reasons for the delay and add these reasons as an enclosure to the record. Applications from Reserve Component personnel will be processed and forwarded to HQDA within 180 days from the date submitted. If processing of an application exceeds 180 days, the GCMCA will state the reasons for the delay for the record, and add these reasons as an enclosure to the record.

c. The person's chain of command will ensure that—

(1) The application is processed expeditiously.

(2) All persons involved in the application process are familiar with their respective responsibilities.

2–2. Advising applicants

a. At the time applicants submit their application, commanders receiving their application will advise them of the pertinent provisions of 5 USC 552a as set forth in figure 2–2. Commanders will inform applicants that the advice applies to all successive steps in the application process, including interviews and solicited written statements. After being advised, applicants will sign and date the statement at figure 2–2. It will then be made part of their application.

b. Commanders will ensure that persons requesting conscientious objector status (1–0) and discharge are advised concerning 38 USC 3103. That section provides that the discharge of persons on the grounds that they are conscientious objectors who refuse to perform military duty, wear the uniform, or otherwise comply with lawful orders of competent military authority, will bar all their rights under the laws administered by the Department of Veterans' Affairs (DVA). (These members will not be barred from their rights to certain types of Government insurance.) Personnel rights will be barred based on the period of service from which the member is discharged or dismissed. However, exceptions may be made by the administrator of the DVA if the member is determined to have been insane. After being so advised, the applicant must sign and date the statement at figure 2–3. The statement will be made part of the application.

c. A person requesting classification as a conscientious objector, noncombatant (1–A–0), will be advised as to the possible consequences concerning enlistment, reenlistment, or extension in accordance with figure 2–1. He or she must sign and date the statement that will be made part of the application.

d. During the processing of the application, substantial delay may be incurred by the person's failure to meet appointments, submit statements, and so forth. If so, the commander will inform the person that such delay prevents the Army from taking action on the request and may contribute to an unfavorable decision when the cause of the delay indicates insincerity on the part of the applicant. Any delay caused by the applicant exceeding 15 days should be made a matter of record.

e. After the application has been received by the person's commander, the commander will arrange for the applicant to be interviewed as soon as possible by a military chaplain and a psychiatrist. The commander will provide the chaplain a copy of the application for his or her review before the interview.

SUBJECT: Counseling Statement

(To whom it may concern)

STATEMENT

I have been counseled concerning designation as a conscientious objector. Based on my training and belief, I consider myself to be a conscientious objector within the meaning of regulations governing conscientious objectors. I am conscientiously opposed to participation in combatant training and service. I request assignment to noncombatant duties for the remainder of my term of service. I fully understand that, on expiration of my current term of service, I may not be eligible for voluntary enlistment, reenlistment, extension, or amendment of current enlistment, or active service in the Armed Forces by reason of my 1-A-O classification.

(signature
applicant's name, grade, SSN
and organization)

Figure 2-1. Statement of Understanding, Noncombatant Status

(date)

SUBJECT: Privacy Act Advice

(To whom it may concern)

I have been advised that in accordance with the Privacy Act of 1974 (5 USC 552a), as implemented by AR 340-21--

a. The authority for requesting disclosure of the information is section 3012, title 10, United States Code.

b. The purpose for requesting disclosure of the information is to provide a basis for acting on the application.

c. The information is used routinely to--

(1) Locate and retrieve pertinent records and information.

(2) Evaluate the merit of the applicant's claim.

(3) Annotate records to reflect results of action taken.

d. Disclosure of the information is voluntary; however, failure to provide information may be cause for denying the requested action, or may make processing of the application impossible.

(signature
applicant's name, grade, SSN
and organization)

Figure 2-2. Statement of Understanding, Privacy Act

(date)

SUBJECT: Section 3103, Title 38,
United States Code

(To whom it may concern)

I have been advised of the provisions of 38 USC 3103 concerning my possible nonentitlement to benefits administered by the Veterans Administration (VA) if I am discharged from the military service as a conscientious objector under certain conditions. I understand that a discharge as a conscientious objector, who refused to perform military duty, wear the uniform, or otherwise to comply with lawful orders of competent military authority will bar all my rights under any laws administered by the VA. I understand nonentitlement is based upon the period of service from which I was discharged. My legal entitlement (if any) to any war risk, Government (converted), or National Service Life Insurance, I understand, is an exception to this policy.

(signature
applicant's name, grade, SSN
and organization)

Figure 2–3. Statement of Understanding, 38 USC 3103

SUBJECT: Waiver of Appearance at a Hearing
 by the Investigating Officer

(To whom it may concern)

I hereby acknowledge that I have been offered the chance to appear at a hearing on my application for conscientious objector status. I have decided, of my own free will, not to accept this offer and hereby waive the hearing.

(signature
applicant's name, grade, SSN
and organization)

Figure 2–4. Statement, Waiver of Hearing

SUBJECT: Conscientious Objector Hearing

(To whom it may concern)

I, ..., have had explained to me and understand the matters below pertaining to this hearing:

1. The purpose of the hearing is to--
   a. Afford me, as the applicant, a chance to present any evidence in support of this application.
   b. Enable the investigating officer to ascertain and assemble all relevant facts.
   c. Create a comprehensive record.
   d. Facilitate an informed recommendation by the investigating officer and decision by higher authority.

2. If I fail without good cause to appear, or if I refuse to appear at the hearing, the investigating officer may proceed in my absence and I will be deemed to have waived my appearance. I further understand that if I fail or refuse to take an oath, or make an affirmation, as to the truthfulness of my testimony at the hearing, the investigating officer may consider this failure or refusal to take an oath or make an affirmation in making his or her recommendation and evaluation of my request.

3. This hearing may be delayed for good cause at my request.

4. I am entitled to be represented by counsel at no expense to the Government. I do/do not plan to obtain such counsel (appropriately line out and initial).

5. This hearing is not governed by the rules of evidence employed by court-martial, except that all oral evidence will be under oath or affirmation. Any relevant information may be received. Statements received from persons not present need not be under oath or affirmation.

6. This is not an adversary proceeding.

7. I may submit any additional evidence I desire, and present any witnesses in my behalf. However, I must secure their attendance.

8. I am permitted to question any witnesses who appear.

9. A verbatim record of the hearing is not required. However, I may make such a record at no expense to the government. If I do so, I must make a copy available to the investigating officer.

10. The version of the hearing as recorded by the investigating officer is final as to the testimony of the witnesses. However, its regularity may be rebutted.

11. A copy of the record will be forwarded to me at the time the record is forwarded to the commander. I understand that I have the right to submit a rebuttal within 10 calendar days of my receipt of record.

(investigating officer, grade, branch)   *(applicant's name, grade, SSN and organization)*

(applicant's counsel and address if civilian attorney)

Figure 2–5. Statement of Understanding, Hearing on Application

(date)

SUBJECT: Rebuttal Rights

(To whom it may concern)

I, ..., have received a copy of the record of my application, complete through (date) . . . . A statement in rebuttal to the reports, comments, and recommendations in the record is inclosed/ waived (appropriately line-out and initial).

(signature
applicant's name, grade, SSN
and organization)

Figure 2–6. Statement, Rebuttal Rights

(date)

SUBJECT: Voluntary Withdrawal of Conscientious
         Objector Application

(To whom it may concern)

    I, ..., have been counseled by the Judge Advocate officer named below concerning my rights as a conscientious objector applicant. I have decided of my own free will to withdraw my application at this time. This withdrawal is not the result of any inducement or coercion.

*(applicant's name, grade, SSN
and organization)*

    I, ..., have counseled the applicant as indicated above. The applicant appeared to understand his or her rights and to act voluntarily, without reservation.

Witnessed this . . . day of . . ., 19 . . .

*(Judge Advocate General's Corps officer's name,
grade, and organization*

Figure 2–7. Statement, Waiver of Application

2–3. Interviewing applicants

a. The interviewing chaplain may be from any component of the Armed Forces but not assigned to an Active or Inactive Control Group.

(1) Before interviewing applicants, the chaplain will advise them that any communication between the applicant and the chaplain will *not* be privileged since a detailed report of the interview will become a part of the application for consideration in the adjudication process. Thus, if the applicant has established a relationship of confidentiality (counseling) with a chaplain, a different chaplain will conduct the interview. This provision does not prevent an applicant from soliciting a letter to support the claim from anyone he or she chooses.

(2) The interviewing chaplain will submit a detailed report of the interview to the commander. This report will include comments on the following:

(*a*) Nature and basis of the person's claim.

(*b*) Opinion on the source of the beliefs.

(*c*) Sincerity and depth or lack of conviction.

(*d*) Appropriate comments of the person's demeanor and lifestyle as they bear on the claim.

(*e*) Specific reasons for the chaplain's conclusions.

(*f*) If it is felt that the applicant is insincere in his or her beliefs or his or her lifestyle is incongruent with the claim, statements to this effect should be documented in this report.

(*g*) If the applicant refuses to be interviewed by a chaplain, the chaplain will submit a report explaining the circumstances. Appropriate comments on the applicant's demeanor as it bears on the claim will be included.

(*h*) No recommendation for approval or disapproval of the application will be made by the chaplain.

b. The applicant will also be interviewed by a psychiatrist (or other medical officer if a psychiatrist is not available) who may be from any component of the Armed Forces. The psychiatrist will submit a mental status examination report indicating the presence or absence of any psychiatric disorder that would warrant treatment or disposition through medical channels, or such a personality disorder as to warrant recommendation for appropriate administrative action. No information obtained from the applicant, during the evaluation, or any matter derived from the evaluation, will be made available outside medical channels except as needed for processing the person for further mental evaluation or discharge for medical reasons. Results of the evaluation will be recorded on DA Form 3822–R (Report of Mental Status Evaluation) (AR 635–200, fig 1–3). The form will be annotated in the remarks section to reflect that the person has applied for conscientious objector status. Upon completion, this form will be given to the person's commander to become part of the application. If the applicant refuses mental evaluation or is uncooperative or unresponsive during the interview, this fact will be included in the report. The psychiatrist or medical officer will make no recommendation for approval or disapproval of the application.

2–4. Investigating applicants' claim

a. The applicant's commander will forward the application, the chaplain's report of interview, and the report of mental status examination to the commander exercising special court–martial jurisdiction over the person. The latter commander will appoint an officer, grade O–3 or higher, knowledgeable in policies and procedures relating to conscientious objection, to investigate the person's claim. The appointing orders will be made part of the case record.

b. The investigating officer so appointed—

(1) Will neither be a person in the applicant's chain of command, nor one who has the primary responsibility for making recommendations on administrative matters to the commander.

(2) Should not be from the same company or battery–size unit, but may be from the same battalion–size unit.

(3) Must be senior in grade to the person if the person is a commissioned officer.

c. Commanders of supporting installations, as defined in AR 5–9, will provide assistance upon the request of the CG, USAHRC–St. Louis, to arrange for necessary interviews of nonunit Reservists residing in their geographical area of jurisdiction.

d. Upon appointment, the investigating officer will—

(1) Review the application.

(2) Study the applicable Army regulations.

(3) Obtain legal advice from the local SJA or other command legal officer as necessary prior to submitting a written report.

(4) Seek information from commanders, supervisors, records, and any other sources that may contribute to his or her final recommendation.

(5) Request the applicant's Selective Service System records, or specific information contained in these records, if he or she believes such a review of the records or such specific information is needed for a complete inquiry.

(6) When the applicant indicates that an application for conscientious objector status was previously denied by an armed service or by the Selective Service System, obtain and review the records of that prior application.

e. All local Selective Service System board records have been retired to Federal record centers. Any request for records or information from the Selective Service System must be accompanied by the applicant's release authorization for HQDA to obtain the information, if available. This release authorization, signed and dated by the applicant, will be sent to the address specified in paragraph 2–8*c*. It will contain as a minimum the following information pertaining to the applicant:

(1) Full name.

(2) Date of birth.

(3) Selective Service System number.

(4) Social security number.

f. The information obtained from the Selective Service System will be presented to the applicant at the hearing or later. It will be made a part of the record.

2–5. Conducting investigations

a. The investigating officer will conduct a hearing on the application. The person will be notified in writing as to the time and place the hearing will be held. The person's receipt of the notice should be acknowledged by his or her signature and the date of the receipt on the letter of notification. A copy of the notification will be attached to the hearing record.

b. The hearing may be delayed for good cause at the person's request. However, if the person fails to appear at the stated time and place for the hearing, the person will be deemed to have waived his or her appearance and the investigating officer may proceed in the person's absence. If the person fails to appear through no fault of his or her own, the hearing will be rescheduled.

c. The person may not wish a hearing on his or her application. If so, the person may waive his or her right to a hearing by executing a statement to the effect at figure 2–4.

d. The execution of a waiver of a hearing does not waive the requirement for an investigating officer. Regardless of the desires of the person, an investigating officer will be appointed to comply with the requirements described in this regulation.

e. The purpose of the hearing is to—

(1) Give the person an opportunity to present any evidence he or she desires to support the application.

(2) Enable the investigating officer to ascertain and assemble all relevant facts.

(3) Create a comprehensive record that aids the investigating officer and other decisionmakers in arriving at informed recommendations.

f. At the beginning of the hearing, the investigating officer will require the person to acknowledge his or her understanding of the nature of the hearing, as stated in figure 2–5, by signing and dating the same.

g. The hearing will be informal. It will not be governed by the rules of evidence employed by a court–martial, except that all oral testimony presented will be under oath or affirmation. Any failure or refusal by the person to submit to questioning under oath or affirmation before the investigating officer may be considered in the recommendation and evaluation of the person's claim. Any relevant evidence may be received. However, statements obtained from persons not present at the hearing need not be notarized or sworn. The use of DA Form 1574 (Report of Proceedings by Investigating Officer/Board of Officers) in the conduct of the hearing is not recommended. The hearing is not an adversary proceeding.

h. The applicant may submit any additional evidence desired, including sworn and unsworn statements. He or she may also present any witnesses, but must secure their attendance. The installation or local commander will render all reasonable assistance in making available military members of the command requested by the applicant as witnesses. Further, the applicant will be permitted to question any other witnesses who appear and to examine all items in the file. A chaplain may feel that his or her appearance might lead to a violation of AR 165–1. If so, the investigating officer will not require a chaplain, other than the interviewing chaplain (para 2–3*a*), to appear at a hearing.

i. If the applicant desires, he or she is entitled to be represented by counsel at no expense to the Government. The counsel will be allowed to attend and participate in all hearings and to assist the applicant in presentation of the case. The counsel will also be allowed to examine all items in the case file.

j. A verbatim record of the hearing is not required; however, if the applicant desires such a record and agrees to provide it at his or her own expense, he or she may do so. If the applicant elects to provide such a record, a copy will be made available to the investigating officer, at no expense to the Government, at the conclusion of the hearing. In the absence of a verbatim record, the investigating officer will summarize the testimony of witnesses. The investigating officer will permit the applicant or counsel to examine the summaries and note, for the record, the differences with the investigating officer's summary. Copies of statements and other documents received in evidence will be made a part of the hearing record. The investigating officer will authenticate the hearing record. The investigating officer's version is final as to the record of the testimony of the witnesses.

k. At the end of the investigation, the investigating officer will prepare a written report in 4 copies. The report will contain the items below—

(1) A properly executed statement of understanding (fig 2–5).

(2) A properly executed statement of waiver (fig 2–4) if the applicant chose to waive his or her right to a hearing by the investigating officer.

(3) Any documents, statements, and other material received in evidence during the investigation.

(4) Summaries of the testimony of the witnesses presented (or a verbatim record of the testimony if such record was made).

(5) A statement of the investigating officer's conclusions as to—

(*a*) The underlying basis of the person's professed conscientious objection (what applicant believes, and why).

(*b*) The time period (being as specific as possible) in which the person's belief became fixed.

(*c*) Whether the belief constitutes conscientious objection (1–0 or 1–A–0) under this regulation.

(*d*) The sincerity of the person, including reasons for such conclusions.

(6) The investigating officer's recommendation for disposition of the case. Reasons (basis in fact and not conjecture) for the recommendations will be included. The actions recommended will be limited to the following:

(*a*) Denial of any classification as a conscientious objector.

(*b*) Classification as 1–A–0 conscientious objector.

(*c*) Classification as 1–0 conscientious objector.

(7) In 1–0 application cases, the investigating officer will not recommend a classification of (1–A–0) unless the

person has indicated a willingness to remain on active duty in a noncombatant role. If such an indication is present, the investigating officer should obtain a written statement from the person that affirms the willingness to serve.

(8) In (1–A–0) application cases, the investigating officer will not recommend discharge (1–0) since the person has stated a willingness to serve as a noncombatant. This willingness shows that the person does not object to participation in war in any form.

l. The investigating officer's conclusions and recommended disposition will be based on the entire record, not merely on the evidence produced at the hearings.

m. The investigating officer's report along with the person's application, all interviews with chaplains and doctors, evidence received as a result of the hearing, and any other items submitted by the person to support the application make up the case record. A copy of the case record will be forwarded to the person at the same time that the original is forwarded to the commander who appointed the investigating officer. The person has the right to submit a rebuttal statement to the record within 10 calendar days. After receipt of the record, the person will complete the statement acknowledging rebuttal rights as prescribed in figure 2–6, along with a rebuttal statement, when appropriate. The person will deliver the statement(s) to his or her immediate unit commander within 10 days of his or her receipt of the record. The headquarters of the appointing commander will return the case record without comment to the person's immediate commander for the information required by paragraph 2–6a.

2–6. Review of cases

a. The unit commander will take the actions below after he or she has received the statement prescribed in figure 2–6, and any statement(s) in rebuttal, if appropriate, from the applicant or after the 10 calendar days' rebuttal time allowed the applicant has expired—

(1) Include the information below on DA Form 4187 as comment 2; forward the application through channels.

(a) Whether approval or disapproval is recommended with supporting reasons.

(b) Duty and primary military occupational specialty (MOS) of the applicant.

(c) Whether medical board or physical evaluation board proceedings are pending or appropriate.

(d) Whether the person is under investigation, under charges, awaiting result of trial, absent without leave, or under suspension of favorable personnel action according to AR 600–8–2. Applications for conscientious objector status submitted by persons who are under suspension of favorable personnel actions under AR 600–8–2 will include, from the proper commander, a detailed account of the events that prompted the initiation of the suspension.

(2) Add the completed figure 2–6 statement of the person to the record along with rebuttal statement, if executed.

b. If the person has no unit commander, the custodian of the person's MPRJ will take the actions required by *a,* above.

c. The record of the case will then be forwarded through command channels, for recommendations as to disposition of the case (based on fact and not conjecture), to the GCMCA who will review the case for administrative correctness. The GCMCA review will ensure that all of the regulatory requirements have been expeditiously and properly completed in the required number of copies. If there has been undue delay in processing the application, the headquarters of general court–martial jurisdiction will comply with paragraph 2–1b.

d. After the administrative review, the case record will be forwarded to the SJA of the GCMCA. The SJA will review the case for sufficiency in law and fact. The SJA will ensure that the applicant has been afforded the procedural safeguards of this regulation. The SJA will make a recommendation for disposition of the case, supported by reasons. The use of only the term "legally sufficient" does not fulfill this requirement. Comments by judge advocates below the GCMCA level are gratuitous but, if made, will be addressed by higher headquarters when a conflicting recommendation is made.

e. The case may be returned to the investigating officer if further investigation is deemed necessary; however, all original documents will remain in the case record. New or revised documents may be added to the case record but not substituted for the originals. At the conclusion of an additional investigation, a new recommendation may be made, if appropriate. If new information adverse to the person is added to the record, or if a new recommendation is made, it will be forwarded to the applicant for rebuttal. The person will execute a new rebuttal form (fig 2–6) at this time. The case record, with the new material added, will be forwarded through command channels to the headquarters that initiated the request for further investigation.

2–7. Voluntary withdrawal of application

A person may desire to withdraw his or her application before final action has been taken. If so, he or she should notify the immediate unit commander, or records custodian (see para 2–6b) of his or her decision. Upon such notice, the following actions will be taken:

a. The immediate unit commander will arrange for the person to be counseled by an officer of The Judge Advocate General's Corps (JAGC).

b. The JAGC officer will advise the person of his or her legal rights in the matter and execute, with the person, the statement in figure 2–7 concerning voluntary withdrawal of such application.

c. The entire application, to include the voluntary withdrawal statement, will be forwarded in 2 copies directly to HQDA as outlined in paragraph 2–8*c.*

2–8. Decision authority

a. Approval of application. Authority to approve applications for noncombatant conscientious objector status (1–A–0) is delegated to the commander exercising GCMCA over the applicant and the proper level of command listed below for the Reserve Component. The DACORB will make the final determination on all applications requesting discharge (1–0) and those requesting noncombatant status (1–A–0) that are not approved by the command level listed below—.

(1) Applications submitted by Army personnel on active duty will be forwarded through normal command channels to the Active Army commander having GCMCA for recommendations with supporting reasons (1–0 and disapproval of 1–A–0), or determination and action on approved applications (1–A–0). These applications will include those for personnel in the Army National Guard (ARNG) and U.S. Army Reserve (USAR) on active duty or active duty for training (ADT).

(2) Applications submitted by ARNG personnel who are not on active duty or ADT will be forwarded through normal command channels to the State Adjutant General for—

(a) Recommendations with supporting reasons (1–0 and disapproval of 1–A–0), or

(b) Determination and action on approved applications (1–A–0).

(3) Applications submitted by USAR unit personnel and those nonunit personnel under the jurisdiction of an oversea area commander who are not on active duty or ADT will be forwarded through normal command channels to the numbered Armies in the continental United States (CONUSA) or oversea area commander, as applicable, for recommendations with supporting reasons (1–0 and disapproval of 1–A–0) or determination and action on approved applications (1–A–0).

(4) Personnel under the jurisdiction of the commander, USAHRC–St. Louis, who are not on active duty or ADT, will submit their applications to Commander, USAHRC–St. Louis, 1 Reserve Way, St. Louis, MO 63132–5200. They will request recommendations with supporting reasons (1–0 and disapproval of 1–A–0) or determination and action on approved applications (1–A–0).

b. Delegating authority. Commanders cited in *a,* above are not authorized to further delegate this authority without prior approval of the Secretary of the Army. The GCMCA commanders listed in *a,* above must personally sign each action.

c. Disposition of approved case (1–A–0 only). Two copies of the completed record of a case, approved by the authority in *a,* above, will be forwarded directly to HQDA (DAPE–MPC–CO), Hoffman II, 200 Stovall Street, Alexandria, VA 22332 for proper disposition and review of the application for compliance with HQDA policies and procedures.

d. Disposition of applications for discharge or applications recommended for disapproval.

(1) Four copies of applications requesting discharge (1–0), or applications (1–A–0) not approved by the command levels in *a,* above, will be forwarded directly to HQDA (DAPE–MPC–CO), Hoffman II, 200 Stovall Street, Alexandria, VA 22332. The authority in *a,* above, before forwarding a case wherein disapproval is recommended to HQDA, will furnish the person a copy of the disapproval recommendation and the supporting reasons. The applicant will execute the rebuttal rights statement in figure 2–6. The applicant's comments, if provided, and the figure 2–6 statement will be attached to the record. The command will make no surrebuttal or further substantive comment.

(2) The HQDA (DAPE–MPC–CO) will furnish the proper authority appropriate disposition instructions for applications approved by HQDA.

(3) If a determination by HQDA that the person's request is disapproved, the reasons for this decision will be made a part of the record. It will be provided to the person through command channels.

2–9. Second and later applications

a. An application for discharge as a conscientious objector (1–0) or for classification (1–A–0) that has been considered and disapproved by HQDA will not be reconsidered. However, an applicant may submit second and later formal applications to his or her unit commander. These applications will be considered *only* if—

(1) They are not based upon substantially the same grounds, or

(2) They are not supported by substantially the same evidence, as a previously disapproved application.

b. When a second or later formal application is received, the unit commander will forward the application and any documents submitted with it to the headquarters of the GCMCA specified in paragraph 2–8*a.* At this headquarters the SJA will review the application to determine whether it is substantially the same as a previous application disapproved by HQDA. After the legal review and opinion, the approval authorities specified in paragraph 2–8*a* are authorized to return to a person, without action, any second or later application under this regulation when review reveals that it is substantially the same as a previous application disapproved by HQDA.

c. If the GCMCA specified in paragraph 2–8*a,* by means of the legal review and opinion, determines that the second or later application is not substantially the same as a previously disapproved application, the GCMCA will return the application to the person's unit commander to process according to this regulation. A new chaplain's report of interview and mental status evaluation or a psychiatric evaluation, and a new investigating officer's report also is required.

d. If the final decision to approve or disapprove is not authorized to be made at the GCMCA level, the application will be forwarded to HQDA (see para 2–8*c*) for final action.

2–10. Use, assignment, and training

a. Except as provided in *b,* below, persons who have submitted applications (see para 2–1) will be retained in their unit and assigned duties providing minimum practicable conflict with their asserted beliefs, pending a final decision on their applications. Reassignment orders received after the submission of an application will be delayed until the approval authority makes a final determination. In the case of trainees, they will not be required to train in the study, use, or handling of arms or weapons. The trainee is not precluded from taking part in those aspects of training that do not involve the bearing or use of arms, weapons, or munitions. Except for this restriction, conscientious objector applicants are subject to all military orders and discipline, and regulations to include those on training.

b. In the case of second and later applications, the duty limitations of *a,* above, will not apply if the applicant's immediate commander determines that the application is substantially the same as a previously disapproved application. However, the provisions of paragraph 2–9 still apply.

c. Guidelines for Soldiers submitting an application for conscientious objection is as follows:

(1) A Soldier assigned or attached to a unit deploying to a new duty station (new duty location is the final destination of the deploying unit) may submit an application for conscientious objector status. The Soldier's submission of a conscientious objector application will not preclude the Soldier from deploying with his or her unit. The unit will process the application as operational mission requirements permit. The Soldier will prepare for deployment and deploy with the unit unless the application for conscientious objector status has been approved by the approving authority designated in paragraph 2–8*a.* In cases where a Soldier's application has been forwarded to the DACORB, the commander exercising general court–martial convening authority over the Soldier may, in his discretion, excuse the Soldier from deployment, pending decision of the DACORB.

(2) A Soldier who received individual orders for reassignment prior to submission of conscientious objector application or a Soldier who has departed his or her unit of assignment in compliance with individual reassignment orders may not apply for conscientious objector status until he or she arrives at the new permanent duty station. The foregoing does not apply to Soldiers who are on temporary duty en route on assignment orders for a period in excess of 8 weeks. These Soldiers may apply at their temporary duty location.

d. When a request for conscientious objector status has been denied, the person—

(1) Will comply with reassignment orders, and

(2) May be assigned to any duties, or

(3) May be required to participate in any type of training.

e. In the case of Reserve Component personnel not on active duty, the submission of an application after the date the applicant's orders are published, announcing a reporting date for active duty or ADT is not a basis for delay in reporting for designated duty. If a person is ordered to report to active duty or ADT while an application is being processed and he or she is advised that final action cannot be made before the reporting date for duty, he or she must comply with these orders. In such instance, the application will be forwarded to the proper Active Army GCMCA for processing.

f. Individual Ready Reserve members who have been ordered to active duty may submit an application for conscientious objector status at their mobilization site. Submission of an application will not preclude further assignment or deployment. Upon departure from the mobilization site, the Soldier will hand–carry the application packet if it has not been forwarded to the DACORB. If application has been forwarded to the DACORB, the Soldier's forwarding address (if known) will be included.

g. Notwithstanding the retention requirements stated above, an application for conscientious objector status will be transferred to the gaining commander for appropriate action. This is true for an application submitted by a Soldier who is confined as a result of a court–martial sentence and transferred to a correctional holding detachment according to AR 190–47.

2–11. Guidelines for processing conscientious objector cases

See appendix C for suggested checklist for processing conscientious objector applications.

Chapter 3
Disposition of Personnel

3–1. Action after approval

a. Persons determined to meet the criteria for (1–0) classification normally will be discharged "for the convenience of the Government."

(1) *Active duty personnel (officers, warrant officers, and enlisted).* Orders directing persons to report to a transfer activity designated to accomplish discharge processing will cite this regulation as the authority for discharge and the proper separation program designator (SPD) from AR 635–5–1.

(2) *Reserve Component personnel not on active duty or active duty training.* Orders announcing discharge will cite this regulation as the authority.

(3) *Department of Defense–sponsored educational programs.* When applicable, the Soldier must reimburse the Government for any unearned bonus or special pay and unearned portions of appropriated funds expended on him or her under Department of Defense (DOD)–sponsored educational programs in accordance with proper public law (PL 92–426; PL 95–57) or other DOD directives.

b. Persons who are classified (1–A–0) are not eligible for discharge under this regulation.

(1) *Active duty personnel.* Persons classified (1–A–0) will be identified by an entry on the person's Personnel Qualification Record, Part II (DA Form 2–1) as provided by AR 600–8–104. Enlisted personnel will be assigned according to AR 614–20, and this regulation. Commissioned officers and warrant officers will be designated and used in a proper noncombat–arms specialty and precluded from unit assignments in which they are required to bear arms or to be trained in their use.

(2) *Reserve Component personnel.* Persons classified (1–A–0) will be identified in accordance with (1), above. Such persons will be required to complete their Ready Reserve and statutory obligation or terms of enlistment subject to assignment instructions outlined in this regulation.

(a) Ready Reserve Soldiers will be—

1. Continued in current Reserve assignment if such assignment qualifies as noncombatant service and training; or

2. Assigned to a proper vacancy in a Reserve medical unit, if available; or

3. Assigned to an annual training or reinforcement control group, whichever is appropriate, under criterion pre-scribed in AR 140–10.

(b) Standby Reserve Soldiers will be continued in current assignment.

(c) Army National Guard of the United States Soldiers who, upon separation from their state status as ARNG and/or upon withdrawal of Federal recognition, revert to USAR status will be assigned in accordance with *(a)2* or *(a)3*, above.

c. A copy of the approved case record will be forwarded to Commander, EREC (ATTN: PCRE–FS), 8899 E. 56th Street, Indianapolis, IN 46249–5301, for enlisted personnel; or CDR, HRC (ATTN: AHRC–MSR), 200 Stovall Street, Alexandria, VA 22332–0444, for officer personnel. The copy will be filed in the OMPF in accordance with AR 600–8–104.

3–2. Discharge of personnel having less than 180 days service

Personnel who have less than 180 days on active duty (excluding ADT) may be discharged by reason of conscientious objection. If so, the Selective Service System, National Headquarters, Arlington, VA 22209–2425, will be notified promptly of the date of discharge from military service and advised that the person has not completed 180 days active duty.

3–3. Removal of identification as 1–A–0 conscientious objector

When a person who has been classified as a conscientious objector under this regulation desires to have identification (1–A–0) removed, the procedures below will apply—

a. The person will submit a request to his or her commanding officer. DA Form 4187 or a letter will be prepared in 4 copies. All copies will be signed. The request will contain a statement that the applicant is no longer a conscientious objector and is not opposed to combat duty. A statement will also be made as to why the classification (1–A–0) is no longer applicable. If applicable, the request will contain the person's Selective Service number, local board number, and address.

b. The unit commander, after making a determination that the applicant is sincere, will approve the request and forward it to the custodian of records. The custodian will then delete the conscientious objector entry on the person's qualification record (DA Form 2–1). Action will also be taken to delete this identification from any data processing records on which the classification may be coded. The custodian will indicate by comment on all copies of the DA Form 4187 when the entry on the DA Form 2–1 has been deleted. He or she will distribute the copies as follows—

(1) Original to be filed as a permanent document in the person's MPRJ.

(2) Copy to be forwarded to HQDA (DAPE–MPC–CO), Room 5S15, Hoffman II, 200 Stovall Street, Alexandria, VA 22332.

(3) Copy to the Commander, U.S. Army Enlisted Records and Evaluation Center, Fort Benjamin Harrison, IN

46210, for enlisted personnel or Commander, Military Personnel Records Center, Alexandria, VA 22332, for officer personnel, for filing in the OMPF according to AR 600–8–104.

(4) Copy to be returned to the person concerned.

(5) For Soldiers of the USAR and ARNG, copy to be forwarded through channels to the proper State Adjutant General or Commander, USAHRC.

3–4. Separation certificates

a. An Honorable Discharge Certificate (DD Form 256A) or a General Discharge Certificate (Under Honorable Conditions) (DD Form 257A) will be furnished. Commissioned officers and warrant officers will be furnished a discharge certificate in accordance with AR 600–8–24 or as directed by HQDA. Enlisted personnel will be furnished a discharge certificate in accordance with AR 635–200.

b. DD Form 214 (Certificate of Release or Discharge from Active Duty) will be furnished each person discharged from active service under this regulation.

c. When discharged because of conscientious objection, enter AR 600–43 in item 25 and "RE 4" in item 27 (see AR 635–5–1 for information to be entered in items 26 and 28).

3–5. Expenses

No expenses voluntarily incurred by the person, his or her counsel, his or her witnesses, or by any other person in his or her behalf in connection with proceedings under this regulation will be paid by the Government.

Appendix A
References

Section I
Required Publications

AR 140–10
Assignments, Attachments, Details, and Transfers. (Cited in paragraph 3–1*b*(2)(*a*)3.)

AR 165–1
Chaplain Activities in the United States Army. (Cited in paragraph 2–5*h*.)

AR 600–8–2
Suspension of Favorable Personnel Actions (FLAGs). (Cited in paragraph 2–6*a*(1)(*d*).)

AR 600–8–104
Military Personnel Information Management/Records. (Cited in paragraph 3–1*b*(1).)

AR 635–200
Active Duty Enlisted Administrative Separations. (Cited in paragraphs 1–5*e*, 2–3*b*, and 3–4*a*.)

DODD 1300.6
Conscientious Objectors. (Cited in summary.) (Available at http://www.dtic.mil/whs/directives/corres/dir1.html.)

Section II
Related Publications
A related publication is a source of additional information. The user does not have to read it to understand this regulation.

AR 5–9
Area Support Responsibilities

AR 140–1
Mission, Organization, and Training

AR 190–47
The Army Corrections System

AR 340–21
The Army Privacy Program

AR 600–8–24
Officer Transitions and Discharges

AR 600–8–105
Military Orders

AR 614–20
Enlisted Assignments and Utilization Management

AR 635–5–1
Separation Program Designator (SPD) Codes

PL 92–426
Health Professions Revitalization Act

PL 95–57
A bill to amend Chapter 5 of title 37, United States Code, to extend the special pay provisions for reenlistment, enlistment bonuses

5 USC 552a
Records maintained on individuals

38 USC 3103
Periods of eligibility

50 USC, App 456(j)
Military Selective Service Act

Section III
Prescribed Forms
This section contains no entries.

Section IV
Referenced Forms
This section contains no entries.

Appendix B
Personal Information that Must be Included in Application

B-1.
In accordance with the Privacy Act of 1974 (5 USC 552a), as implemented by AR 340-21, applicants will be advised as outlined in paragraph 2–2a. The Privacy Act form will be signed and become part of the record (fig 2–2). Also, the following will be provided:

a. General information.

(1) Full name.

(2) Social security number.

(3) Selective Service number (if applicable).

(4) Service address and component (Regular Army (RA), USAR, ARNG).

(5) Permanent home address.

(6) Name and address of each school and college attended together with dates of attendance, and the type of school (public, church, military, commercial, and so forth).

(7) A chronological list of all occupations, positions, jobs, or types of work, other than as a student in school or college, whether for monetary compensation or not. Include the type of work, name of employer, address of employer, and the from and to date for each position or job held.

(8) All former addresses and dates of residence at those addresses.

(9) Parent's names and addresses. Indicate whether they are living or deceased.

(10) The religious denomination or sect of both parents.

(11) Was application made to the Selective Service System (local board) for classification as a conscientious objector before entry into the Armed Forces? If so, to which local board? What decision, if any, that was made by the board, if known?

(12) Was any previous application made in service for classification as a conscientious objector? If so, for which status (1–0 or 1–A–O)? Where and when was application made? What was the final determination? Attach a copy of the previous application(s), if any.

(13) When the person has served less than 180 days in the Armed Forces, a statement by him or her as to whether he or she is willing to perform work under the Selective Service civilian work program for conscientious objectors if discharged as a conscientious objector. Also, a statement of the applicant as to whether he or she consents to the issuance of an order for such work by his or her local Selective Service board.

b. Training and belief.

(1) An express, specific statement as to whether the person requests classification as a conscientious objector (1–0), or as a conscientious objector (1–A–0).

(2) A description of the nature of the belief that requires the person to seek separation from the military service or assignment to noncombatant training and duty for reasons of conscience.

(3) An explanation as to how his or her beliefs changed or developed, to include an explanation as to what factors (how, when, and from whom or from what source training received and belief acquired) caused the change in or development of conscientious objection beliefs.

(4) An explanation as to when these beliefs become incompatible with military service and why.

(5) An explanation as to the circumstances, if any, under which the person believes in the use of force, and to what extent, under any foreseeable circumstances.

(6) An explanation as to what in the person's life most conspicuously demonstrates the consistency and depth of his or her beliefs that have rise to his or her claim.

(7) An explanation as to how the applicant's daily lifestyle has changed as a result of his or her beliefs and what future actions he or she plans to continue to support his or her beliefs.

c. Participation in organizations.

(1) Information as to whether the person has ever been a member of any military organization or establishment before entering upon his or her present term of service. If so, the name and address of such organization will be given together with reasons why he or she became a member.

(2) A statement as to whether the person is a member of a religious sect or organization. If so, the statement will show—

(a) The name of the sect, and the name and location of its governing body or head, if known.

(b) When, where, and how the applicant became a member of the sect or organization.

(c) The name and location of any church, congregation, or meeting that the applicant customarily attends; the extent of the applicant's participation in the church group or meeting.

(d) The name, title, and present address of the pastor or leader of such church, congregation, or meeting.

(e) A description of the creed or official statements, if any, of said religious sector organization in relation to the applicant's participation in war and if the creed or statements are known to him.

(3) A description of the applicant's relationships with and activities in all organizations with which he or she is or has been affiliated, other than military, political, or labor organizations.

d. References. Any more information that the person desires to be considered by the authority reviewing his or her application. Letters of reference or official statements of organizations to which the applicant belongs or refers in his or her application are included. The burden is on the applicant to obtain and forward such information.

B–2.

Each person seeking a discharge from the Army (1–0), or assignment to noncombatant duties (1–A–0), as a conscientious objector under this regulation, will provide the information indicated above as the minimum required for consideration of his or her request. However, HQDA may require such additional information as it deems proper. The person may submit such other information as desired.

Appendix C
Suggested Checklist for Processing Conscientious Objector Applications

C–1.

Has the person submitted a signed and dated DA Form 4187 showing whether he or she is requesting discharge or noncombatant status and all data required by appendix B (para 2–1a)?

C–2.

Has the person been advised by his or her unit commander of the pertinent provisions of the Privacy Act; 38 USC 3103; the possible ineligibility for reenlistment; and then signed and dated the proper statement (figs 2–1 and 2–2 or 2–3) and included them in the case record (para 2–2)?

C–3.

Has the person been advised that he or she may submit any data he or she considers relevant with the application (para 2–1a)?

C–4.

Has the unit commander ensured that the person is retained in the unit after submitting an application and is so retained until the application is finally adjudicated? Reassignment orders received after the submission of an application must be delayed until final determination is made by the approving authority (para 2–10).

C–5.

Has the unit commander assigned duties to the person that provide minimum practical conflict with the person's asserted beliefs (para 2–1a)?

C–6.

Has the unit commander made an appointment for an interview with a military chaplain and provided the chaplain with a copy of the application (para 2–2e)?

C–7.

Has the chaplain provided a detailed report that includes—

a. Nature and basis of applicant's claim?

b. Sincerity and depth of conviction?

c. Opinion as to source of applicant's beliefs?

d. Comments on person's demeanor and lifestyle as they bear on the claim?

(*Note:* The chaplain is prohibited from making a recommendation for approval or disapproval) (para 2–3a)).

C–8.

Has the unit commander made an appointment with a psychiatrist or other medical officer, if a psychiatrist is not available, for a mental status examination. The purpose of the examination is to determine the presence or absence of any psychiatric disorder that would warrant treatment or disposition through medical channels.

(*Note:* The medical officer is prohibited from making any recommendation for approval or disapproval) (para 2–3b).

C–9.

Has the unit commander forwarded the case record to date to the Special Court–Martial Convening Authority (para 2–4)?

C–10.

Have all of the above actions been accomplished expeditiously?

C–11.

Has the Special Court–Martial Convening Authority appointed a disinterested investigating officer (O–3 or higher) not in the person's chain of command (para 2–4a)?

C–12.

Has the investigating officer been instructed to ensure proper and complete fulfillment of responsibilities outlined in governing regulations? The investigating officer can receive instruction, assistance, and counsel from such officers as the SJA and the personnel actions officer (para 2–4).

C–13.

Has the investigating officer given the applicant a chance to appear in person at a hearing with, or without, counsel and a reasonable time to obtain counsel, if desired (para 2–5i)?

C–14.

Has the person signed and dated the statement of understanding (fig 2–5)? If applicant waived the opportunity to be heard, a written waiver must be signed, dated, and made part of the record (para 2–5c and fig 2–4).

C–15.

Has the investigating officer—

a. Studied pertinent regulations and the application?

b. Examined the person's military records to determine if application had been made for discharge under other Army regulations, for schools or other assignments and other pertinent data?

c. Talked to the person's peers and superiors concerning the person's demeanor and lifestyle?

d. Corrected on the spot or caused to be corrected noticeable errors or omissions in the case record?

e. Placed the person and all witnesses under oath (or affirmation) during the hearing and so stated in the investigating officer's report?

f. Determined when and how the alleged conscientious objection became fixed or crystallized or determined that the alleged conscientious objection has not become fixed or crystallized?

g. Required the person to authenticate summaries of his or her testimony?

h. Made a recommendation for approval or disapproval and given reasons based on fact?

i. Provided the person a complete copy of the record at the same time the record is returned to the commander who appointed the investigating officer?

j. Fulfilled his or her responsibilities expeditiously?

C–16.

Has the headquarters of the Special Court–Martial jurisdiction returned the record (para 2–5k), complete to date, to the commander of the person for compliance with paragraph 2–6a?

C–17.

Has the person been advised on rebuttal rights and executed figure 2–6 for enclosure in the case record (para 2–5m)?

C–18.

Has the person's commander—

a. Provided all of the data required by paragraph 2–6a as comment 2 to the person's DA Form 4187, to include his or her recommendation and reasons supporting his or her recommendation?

b. Added the completed figure 2–6 statement of the person to the case record along with the person's rebuttal statement, if executed?

c. Forwarded the entire record through normal command channels at the end of the 10 calendar day rebuttal period? If the person has not submitted a statement and figure 2–6 at the end of the 10 days, the commander will make a statement to that effect and forward the case record (para 2–6).

C–19.

Have the commanders in the chain of command made their recommendations based on fact? The endorsement should so indicate (para 2–6c) whether the person was interviewed by a commander.

C–20.

Has the headquarters of General Court–Martial jurisdiction ensured compliance with paragraph 2–1b and prepared the explanation for delay if the application has been held beyond the time limit specified (para 2–6c)?

C–21.

Has the explanation for delay been added to the case record as an enclosure (para 2–1b)?

C–22.

Has the administrative review been completed and the correct number of copies of the application prepared for submission to the DA (para 2–6c)?

C–23.

Has the SJA thoroughly reviewed the entire case record for sufficiency in law and fact and provided a recommended disposition of the case supported by reasons (para 2–6d)?

C–24.

Has the person been counseled by a JAGC officer and properly executed figure 2–7 if the person wishes to withdraw a formal application (para 2–7b)?

C–25.

Has the approved application or the application recommending disapproval been personally signed by the GCMCA with supporting reasons (para 2–8b)?

C–26.

Have the required number of copies been prepared for forwarding to HQDA (paras 2–8c and 2–8d)?

Appendix D
Informal Guide for the Investigating Officer

D–1.

The investigating officer's investigation and hearing is of prime importance in processing a conscientious objector's application. The investigating officer must perform his duties with diligence, understanding, and expedience. He or she must provide an objective and factual report to the chain of command. A careless or misguided investigating officer can cause unwarranted delays or other serious consequences for the applicant or circumstances that may be prejudicial to the interests of the Army, or both.

D–2.

The investigating officer's first responsibility is to ensure that the record contains all available information necessary for the proper decision authority to make an informed decision. To accomplish this, the investigating officer should—

a. Study applicable regulations. Be fully conversant on the requirements, both administrative and substantive. Even with a good general understanding of these matters, the investigating officer can make mistakes if he or she does not follow the technical requirements.

b. Review the application. Attempt to define the basis of the applicant's beliefs. If these beliefs are based on the tenets of a certain religion. The investigating officer should ask questions of the personnel office, other investigating officers of conscientious objector cases (they are different from other investigations), and the SJA.

c. Talk to the person's superiors and peers concerning the person's lifestyle, conduct, efficiency, and general demeanor as they pertain to the person's claim.

d. Check all that has gone before. If someone failed to fulfill his regulatory responsibilities, the investigating officer should correct the error as soon as possible.

e. Read the chaplain's report, which should be part of the application. This report may assist the investigating officer by focusing the inquiry of the hearing.

f. Read the report of mental status examination. If this report shows any basis for medical treatment or for administrative action based on a personality disorder, these matters take precedence. The investigating officer should report this fact to the commander who appointed him or her.

g. State in the report if he or she is convinced that AR 600–43 is being used to effect the administrative separation of a person who does not qualify as a conscientious objector.

h. Should not deny the request of a sincere person who meets the regulatory criteria because of monetary or service obligations under other pertinent regulations (see para 3–1*a*(3)). The fact that an applicant has just received a reenlistment bonus, a commission, or a degree, has no direct bearing on the main issue. If it appears; however, that the applicant delayed his or her application to complete a Government–sponsored educational program, this delay may be grounds for questioning his sincerity, particularly if the applicant seeks 1–0 status (para 2–2*d*).

i. Question the sincerity of the applicant if an applicant has delayed for a significant period of time after the crystallization of his or her beliefs to submit an application.

j. Complete the entire application process expeditiously. An inordinate delay may prevent proper consideration of the merits of the claim.

D–3.

The investigating officer's hearing provides the chance for the investigating officer to explore fully the person's claim.

a. The hearing is informal; however, the investigating officer must be fully prepared beforehand and should conduct the hearing without outside help.

b. At the hearing, the investigating officer should be impartial. The investigating officer is not an advocate, even if the applicant has retained counsel.

c. The investigating officer's role is not to prove that the applicant is not a conscientious objector, but to find and record all factual data that will provide the basis for his opinion that the person is or is not a conscientious objector. The hearing is to provide the person the chance to establish, by "clear and convincing evidence," that he or she is a conscientious objector as defined by this regulation. The investigating officer's recommendation must be based on fact.

D–4.

During the conduct of the entire investigation, the investigating officer should remember that—

a. A conscientious objector under this regulation is a person who is sincerely opposed, because of religious or deeply held moral or ethical (not political, philosophical, or sociological) beliefs, to participating in war in any form (1–0) or to participating as a combatant (including training in tactics or weapons) in war in any form (1–A–0).

b. An applicant's sincere desire to get out of the Army, his or her unit or job is not conscientious objection. Likewise, an applicant's belief that he or she is called to another occupation, even a religious one, is *not* conscientious objection if he or she merely prefers a different life. A conscientious objector is one whose conscience, because of *a*, above, allows him or her no rest or inner peace if he or she is required to fulfill the present military obligation.

c. Conscientious objector beliefs must be held personally by the applicant. Membership in a certain church group is not necessary or sufficient, even if that group professes conscientious objection. The person who belongs to such a group must clearly show that he or she embraces the group's beliefs as his or her own. Similarly, a person cannot base a claim on the beliefs of a friend or relative.

d. A conscientious objector is not necessarily a pacifist. An applicant may be willing to use force to protect himself or herself or his or her family and still be a conscientious objector. However, if he or she is willing to defend the United States, he or she cannot choose when and where.

e. Applicants who held their beliefs before entry into military service, but failed to make these beliefs known, cannot be discharged or reassigned to noncombatant duty. However, those who have undergone a real change or development of belief since entry into military service or who made these beliefs known but were denied classification before entering active duty may be discharged or reassigned to noncombatant duty, as proper. The investigating officer must attempt to determine if the person has undergone a sudden, easily identifiable experience or exposure to new beliefs, or if old beliefs have matured gradually and taken on new meanings in his or her life and, if so, when, where, and under what circumstances or influences.

f. The person being investigated either is or is not a conscientious objector. If the person is a conscientious objector, he or she should be classified as a noncombatant (1–A–0) or discharged (1–0), as appropriate. If the person is not a conscientious objector, he or she has an obligation to complete his or her service contract.

D–5.

Some administrative considerations for the investigating officer.

a. All documents should bear proper signatures and dates.

b. In the case of those discharged as conscientious objectors, the DVA makes a case–by–case determination of eligibility for benefits. For noncombatants, Army policy on reenlistment changes from time to time; there is no automatic bar. Similarly, reclassification (1–A–0) does not automatically call for removal from a promotion list.

c. Consideration of the type of discharge certificate to be awarded is not proper until after the final decision has been made on the disposition of the conscientious objector application.

d. Any previous correspondence by the applicant (with the Selective Service System, the Army, and so forth) concerning conscientious objection should be considered and included in the record.

Glossary

Section I
Abbreviations

AD
active duty

ADT
active duty training

AGR
Active Guard/Reserve

ARNG
Army National Guard

ARNGUS
Army National Guard of the United States

bt
basic training

CG
commanding general

CONUSA
numbered Armies in the Continental United States

DA
Department of the Army

DACORB
Department of the Army Conscientious Objector Review Board

DCS, G–1
Deputy Chief of Staff, G–1

DEP
delayed entry program

DOD
Department of Defense

DVA
Department of Veterans' Affairs

GCM
general court–martial

GCMCA
general court–martial convening authority

HRC
US Army Human Resources Command

HQDA
Headquarters, Department of the Army

IRR
Individual Ready Reserve

JAGC
Judge Advocate General's Corps

MBT
modified basic training

MEPCOM
Military Entrance Processing Command

MEPS
Military Entrance Processing Station

MOS
military occupational specialty

MPRJ
Military Personnel Records Jacket, US Army

OMPF
Official Military Personnel File

RA
Regular Army

RC
Reserve Components

ROTC
Reserve Officers' Training Corps

SJA
Staff Judge Advocate

SPD
separation program designator

SSN
social security number

TDY
temporary duty

USAEREC
U.S. Army Enlisted Records and Evaluation Center

USA HRC
U.S. Army Human Resources Command

USAHRC–St. Louis
U.S. Army Human Resources Command–St. Louis

USAR
U.S. Army Reserve

USC
United States Code

Section II
Terms

Conscientious objection
A firm, fixed and sincere objection to participation in war in any form or the bearing of arms, because of religious training and belief. Unless otherwise specified, the term "conscientious objector" includes both 1–0 and 1–A–0 conscientious objectors.

a. Class 1–A–0 conscientious objector. A member who, by reason of conscientious objection, sincerely objects to participation as a combatant in war in any form, but whose convictions are such as to permit military service in a noncombatant status.

b. Class 1–0 conscientious objector. A member who, by reason of conscientious objection, sincerely objects to participation of any kind in war in any form.

Enlistee
A person who has enlisted in the delayed entry program (DEP), the RA, or the USAR. An applicant became an enlistee after—

a. The oath of enlistment is taken.

b. Applicable portions of DD Form 4 series (Enlistment/Reenlistment Document—Armed Forces of the United States) are signed.

Entry into service
For an inductee, and only for the purpose of conscientious objection, the date upon which the Selective Service System dispatched his or her notice of induction. For all other members, it is the date upon which they took the oath of enlistment or appointment, or signed the enlistment contract (for cadets who have Reserve Officers' Training Corps scholarships).

Inductee
A person who has become a member of the Armed Forces through the operations of the Selective Service System.

Immediate unit commander
The commanding officer of a company, battery, troop, separate detachment or similar unit.

Modified basic training
Training in basic military subjects, excluding training in the bearing or use of ammunition, weapons, or munitions for conscientious objector personnel.

Noncombatant service or noncombatant duties
(1–A–0) (used interchangeably herein).

a. Service in any unit of the Armed Forces that is unarmed at all times.

b. Service in the medical department of any of the Armed Forces, wherever performed.

c. Any other assignment the primary function of which does not require the use of arms in combat if such other assignment is acceptable to the person concerned and does not require him to bear arms or to be trained in their use.

d. Service aboard an armed ship or aircraft or in a combat zone will not be considered to be combatant duty unless the individual concerned is personally and directly involved in the operation of weapons.

Noncombatant training
Any training that is not concerned with the study, use, or handling of arms or weapons.

Nonunit members
Individual Ready Reserve (IRR) and Standby Reserve members as defined in AR 140–1.

Privileged communications
That communication between an applicant and a chaplain or lawyer that, under law, need not be revealed.

Religious training and belief
Belief in an external power or being or deeply held moral or ethical belief, to which all else is subordinate or upon which all else is ultimately dependent, and which has the power or force to affect moral well–being. The external power or being need not be of an orthodox deity, but may be a sincere and meaningful belief which occupies in the life of its possessor a place parallel to that filled by the God of another, or, in the case of deeply held moral or ethical beliefs, a belief held with the strength and devotion of traditional religious conviction. The term "religious training and belief" may include solely moral or ethical beliefs even though the applicant himself may not characterize these beliefs

as "religious" in the traditional sense, or may expressly characterize them as not religious. The term"religious training and belief" does not include a belief that rests solely upon consideration of policy, pragmatism, expediency, or political views. (In attempting to determine whether a conscientious objection to participation in war or combat is founded upon religious training and belief, as defined above, the proper scope of inquiry is whether the person holds the asserted beliefs and whether they are the product of a conscious thought process resulting in such a conviction as to allow the person no choice but to act in accordance with them. Beliefs can be deeply held even though they lack sophistication. Care must be taken to avoid the inference that an applicant who lacks sufficient insight or knowledge to express his or her beliefs clearly does not hold the beliefs, or that they are not "religious" in origin or held with the strength of traditional religious convictions).

Reserve components
The Army National Guard of the United States and the U.S. Army Reserve.

Supporting installation
Army installations on which U.S. Army Reserve organizations are satellited for logistic support.

War in any form
A person who desires to choose the war in which he or she will participate is not a conscientious objector under the regulation. His of her objection must be to all wars rather than a specific war. However, a belief in a theocratic or spiritual war between the powers of good and evil does not constitute a willingness to participate in "war" within the meaning of this regulation.

Section III
Special Abbreviations and Terms
This section contains no entries.

PIN 004328–000

CPSIA information can be obtained at www.ICGtesting.com
Printed in the USA
BVOW10s1047050515

399028BV00011B/125/P

9 781288 893867